BLETCHLEY TO RUGBY

Vic Mitchell and Keith Smith

MP Middleton Press

Front cover: No. 46256 Sir William A. Stanier, F.R.S. of the "Princess Coronation" class races south through Blisworth on 6th September 1958. The original branch to Northampton is on the right. (M.J.Stretton coll.)

Back cover: Network SouthEast livery was to be seen regularly in the south bays at Rugby. EMU no. 321416 is nearest on 19th September 1993 and is about to depart at 11.09 for Euston via Northampton. (M.J.Stretton)

Published June 2007

ISBN 978 1 906008 07 9

© Middleton Press, 2007

Design Deborah Esher
Typesetting Barbara Mitchell

Published by
        Middleton Press
        Easebourne Lane
        Midhurst
        West Sussex
        GU29 9AZ
Tel: 01730 813169
Fax: 01730 812601
Email: info@middletonpress.co.uk
www.middletonpress.co.uk

Printed & bound by Biddles Ltd, Kings Lynn

INDEX

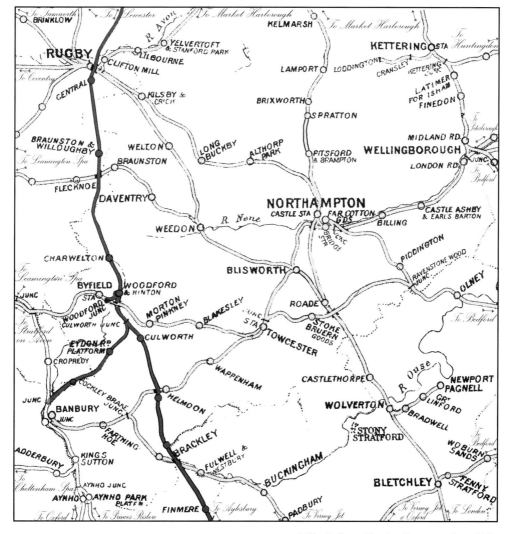

I. The Railway Clearing House map from 1947.

ACKNOWLEDGEMENTS

We are very grateful for the assistance received from many of those mentioned in the credits also to A.R.Carder, L.Crosier, G.Croughton, B.Herbert (Network Rail), B.S.Jennings, D.K.Jones, N.Langridge, J.P.McCrickard, D.H.Mitchell, Mr D. and Dr S.Salter, T.Walsh, E.Wilmshurst and especially our ever supportive wives, Barbara Mitchell and Janet Smith.

GEOGRAPHICAL SETTING

The main line traverses relatively level ground, the first few miles from Bletchley being on Oxford Clay. Thereafter, it is mainly on Limestone and the route was engineered to give gentle gradients, with notable cuttings at Roade and a tunnel north of Welton. Here trains pass through the scarp edge of the northern extension of the Cotswold Hills.

The route through Northampton dips at this important manufacturing centre to cross the Nene Valley. The other river of note to be bridged is the Great Ouse; this is crossed at Wolverton and the Newport Pagnell branch ran close to it.

Our journey starts in Buckinghamshire and passes into Northamptonshire south of Roade. The final three miles are in Warwickshire.

The maps are to the scale of 25ins to 1 mile, with north at the top, unless otherwise indicated.

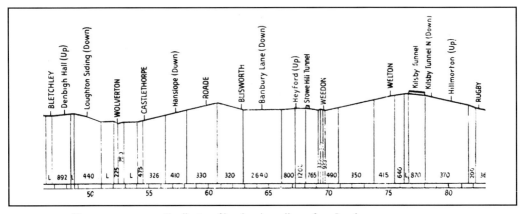

II.   Gradient profiles showing mileage from London.

III.

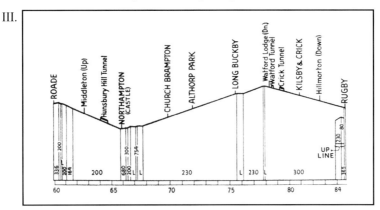

HISTORICAL BACKGROUND

The Act for the London & Birmingham Railway was passed on 6th May 1833 and the line from London to Denbigh Hall (one mile north of Bletchley) was completed (in stages) on 9th April 1838. From there to Birmingham opened on 24th June of that year. A branch from Blisworth to Northampton came on 13th May 1845. The LBR became part of the London & North Western Railway when it was formed on 16th July 1846.

The LNWR opened a line northwards from Northampton to Market Harborough in 1859. The southern two miles of this formed part of a new loop between Roade and Rugby via Northampton, it opening on 1st December 1881. The route south of Roade was quadrupled in readiness for this; completion was in 1879.

Blisworth was the junction for another line from 1866. This was opened by the Northampton & Banbury Junction Railway and it became the Stratford-upon-Avon & Midland Junction Railway in 1910, lasting until 1952. Final years given are for passenger services. This, for the Blisworth to Northampton section, was 1960. There was a westward branch north of Weedon to Leamington Spa. It was open to Daventry between 1888 and 1958.

Quadrupling of the route took place in 1874-81, the new pair of tracks being east of the others and used for slow trains.

Rugby became the hub for a number of lines:
1. 1840-1962 north to Leicester
2. 1847 northwest to Tamworth (open)
3. 1850-1966 east to Market Harborough
4. 1851-1959 southwest to Leamington Spa

No. 1 was part of the Midland Railway in 1844-1923. The Great Central Railway route passed over the London-Rugby main lines, east of the station, between 1898 and 1969. Closure of the Northampton-Market Harborough service took place in 1960, but the line was usable until 1985.

The LNWR became a constituent of the London Midland & Scottish Railway in 1923. Its area formed the London Midland Region of British Railways upon nationalisation in 1948.

Electrification of the LMR main lines began in the North of England and was undertaken with overhead wires at 25,000 volts AC. Electrically hauled freight trains ran south to Willesden Junction from September 1965 and all main line services were electrically operated by 3rd January 1966. The Northampton loop was electrified on 22nd November 1965.

Local services to Northampton came under the control of Network SouthEast on 18th June 1986 and most main line traffic went into the InterCity sector.

The name "North London Railways" was applied from 31st March 1994 to the services to Birmingham via Northampton. These were named Silverlink Trains after privatisation on 2nd March 1997, when a 7½ year franchise was taken by the National Express Group. A week later, Virgin West Coast Trains took over main line operations, with the exception of ScotRail sleeper services, on a 15 year franchise.

Newport Pagnell Branch

The Newport Pagnell Railway was authorised under an Act of 29th June 1863, and one of 1865 gave consent for its extension to Olney. This was started, but never completed. The NPR purchased the canal to the town in 1864 to facilitate construction and to build on its terminal basin.

The branch opened on 2nd September 1867 and was used by many Wolverton Works employees. It was absorbed into the LNWR in 1875.

Passenger service was withdrawn on 7th September 1964, but freight continued until 22nd May 1967.

Wolverton & Stony Stratford Tramway

The 3ft 6ins gauge Wolverton & Stony Stratford Tramway opened on 27th May 1887 and commenced in the goods yard at Wolverton. It was bankrupt in 1889 and again in 1919. The LNWR acquired it in 1920 and provided a Bagnall 0-4-0ST to haul the massive 44ft long 100 seat double deck cars. There were 12 of these in the fleet.

Closure came on 4th May 1926 although the LNWR had relaid the route. This was due to the effect of the General Strike and bus competition. Track removal was completed in 1934.

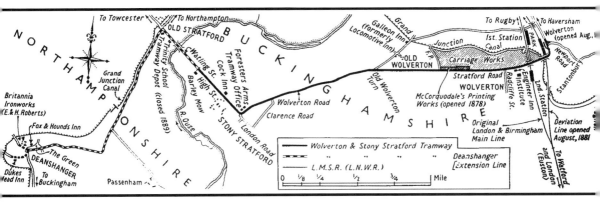

The western terminus for passengers was at the Cock Hotel until about 1910. From 1919, it was at the Foresters Arms. The Deanshanger extension was only in use in 1888-89. (Railway Magazine)

The LNWR's Bagnall was always fitted with a chimney extension and the top decks of the cars had side curtains. This is the terminus at Stony Stratford, not long before closure. The other end of the tramway can be seen in picture 16. (J.C.Gillham coll.)

PASSENGER SERVICES

Down trains serving most intermediate stations on at least five days per week are shown in the following tables. The earlier services are difficult to summarise, as their stopping patterns were very irregular.

	Bletchley to Roade		Northampton to Rugby		Blisworth to Rugby	
	Weekdays	Sundays	Weekdays	Sundays	Weekdays	Sundays
1869	3	1	-	-	12	3
1883	9	1	5	0	10	1
1903	8	1	6	0	4	1
1923	10	3	5	0	7	2
1943	8	2	6	0	3	0
1963	9	2	9	2	-	-

Since electrification, regular interval services have been provided at the remaining stations. A useful Brighton-Rugby hourly train was available in 1997-2002.

The Newport Pagnell branch weekday frequency examples are thus, but no reference to Sunday trains has been found - 1883:9, 1908:10, 1933:14, 1942:9, 1953:9, 1956:7 and 1961:6.

IV.   The 1926 survey at 6 ins to 1 mile has our route at the top and the Oxford to Bedford line from left to right. There were passenger services to Oxford from 1850 to 1967; Bedford trains came in 1846 and still operate. The road across the map had a level crossing over the railway until the station was extensively rebuilt in 1880-81. To the left of it is Bletchley Park, which gained fame after World War II as having been the centre for decoding enemy messages.

1.   A private carriage is on the wagon behind LNWR "Precedent" class no. 2186 *Lowther* waiting to depart south in about 1890. Gas lighting is evident; the LNWR had its own gasworks southeast of the station in the early years, and near the Bedford line later.
(R.S.Carpenter coll.)

V.   The 1880 survey of the northern part of the station includes the three road engine shed and single road carriage shed. The population was under 500 in 1900, but was over 16,000 by 1960. It became part of the new town of Milton Keynes after 1967.

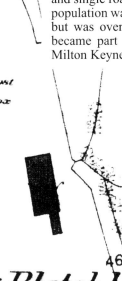

Signal Post
Signal Post

44

5.8

Signal Post
Signal Box

46

48 SOUTH T

Bletchley Station

2.   The stationmasters office is visible in front of no. 6883 on 11th February 1948. It was a Webb design from 1898. The two-storey building is the Station Hotel. (H.C.Casserley)

3.   Standing with the 6.24pm from Watford Junction on the same day is no. 45735 *Comet*, a "Jubilee" class 4-6-0 rebuilt with a larger boiler in 1942 to become class 6P. The engine shed is on the right and the Post Office building is above the loco. (H.C.Casserley)

4.	The engine shed could be seen from the north end of the platforms and the massive water tank is evident beond the column. Nearest are 2-4-2T no. 6687 and 0-8-0 no. 49452. (A.W.V.Mace/ Milepost 92½)

5.	Under repair on 22nd August 1948 is 0-6-2T no. 27561. The shed closed on 15th July 1965 and the site became the car park. (H.C.Casserley)

6.   A 1953 panorama has the hotel on the right and the post office premises in the distance. The booking office is behind the splendid portico and a direct link to the footbridge was created that year. (NRM)

> **Details of the sidings, the flyover with its high level junction and the carriage sheds, both old and new, can be found in our *Oxford to Bletchley* and *Bletchley to Cambridge* albums.**

7.   This view towards London includes the flyover, which was built in 1958-62 for east-west traffic, but was subsequently used very little. The overall roof was soon removed, ready for the electrification scheme. (Lens of Sutton coll.)

8.   Another southward view and this includes one of the 50 class 310 units on 29th November 1984. These were provided for the stopping services between Euston and Birmingham via Northampton when electric services commenced. The canopies are from the 1880s.
(J.C.Gillham)

9.   With the rebuilding came a new entrance, still on the west side. It opened on 13th February 1966 and was recorded on 16th January 1993. (D.A.Thompson)

10.   The platforms were provided with new canopies, except No. 6 (for Bedford) where the steps (far right) were also devoid of shelter. Three class 47s run south with a long freight train on 23rd April 1999. (P.Jones)

DENBIGH HALL

11.   Watling Street was of Roman origin and became the A5 in 1919. By then, it linked London, the Midlands and Holyhead. The location seen was chosen as the temporary terminus of the LBR for eight months, as easy connection with road transport could be made here. The historic inn, seen in 1907, was destroyed in 1958 to allow road widening. (R.M.Casserley coll.)

MILTON KEYNES CENTRAL

12.   The Milton Keynes Development Corporation was established in 1967 and the Lakes Estate, south of Bletchley, was the first area developed. The Open University arrived in 1969, but the station did not open until 14th May 1982. The three photographs were taken two months later. Platform 1 (left) is a bay; its transition to a through line began in 2007. (D.A.Thompson)

13.   The station was built in Central Milton Keynes, hence its name. This is the east elevation of the main complex. H.M.The Queen had opened the Civic Offices, near the shopping centre, in 1979. The through platforms were all designed for 15 coaches. The Wolverton Works train had stopped in this vicinity, near Loughton siding, for employees between at least 1941 and 1952. There were low platforms on the down fast and up slow lines, about two coaches in length. Loughton Goods Siding signal box was on the down side and in use until 15th April 1962. (D.A.Thompson)

14.　　　The entrance hall was intended to serve a population of around 200,000 although there were four other smaller stations within the development area. The A5 was diverted on dual carriageway west of and parallel to the main line, in 1980. (D.A.Thompson)

SOUTH OF WOLVERTON

15.　　　This panorama from about 1908 covers the top part of map VI and has the south end of the triangular junction in the foreground. The works is in the background and Wolverton No.1 signal box is centre. (R.M.Casserley coll.)

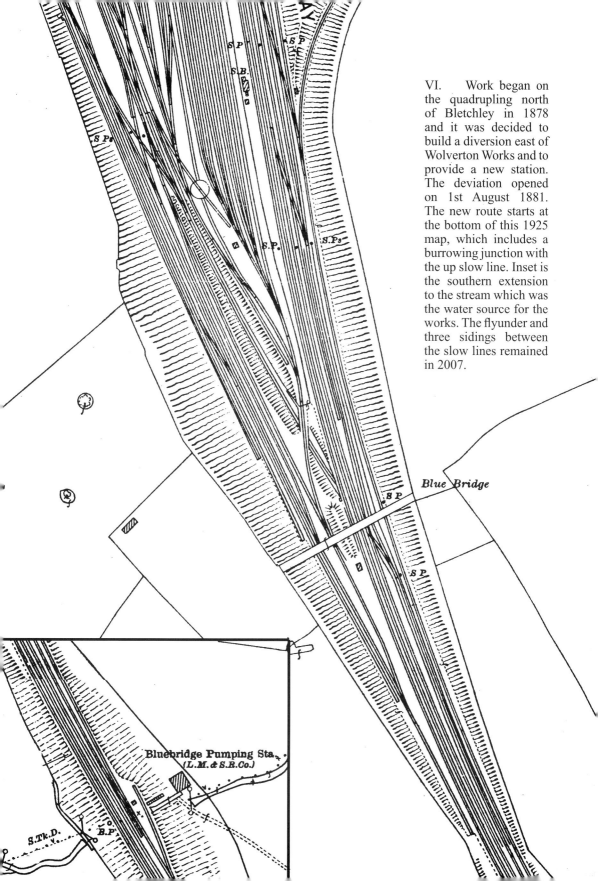

VI. Work began on the quadrupling north of Bletchley in 1878 and it was decided to build a diversion east of Wolverton Works and to provide a new station. The deviation opened on 1st August 1881. The new route starts at the bottom of this 1925 map, which includes a burrowing junction with the up slow line. Inset is the southern extension to the stream which was the water source for the works. The flyunder and three sidings between the slow lines remained in 2007.

Blue Bridge

Bluebridge Pumping Sta.
(L.M. & S.R.Co.)

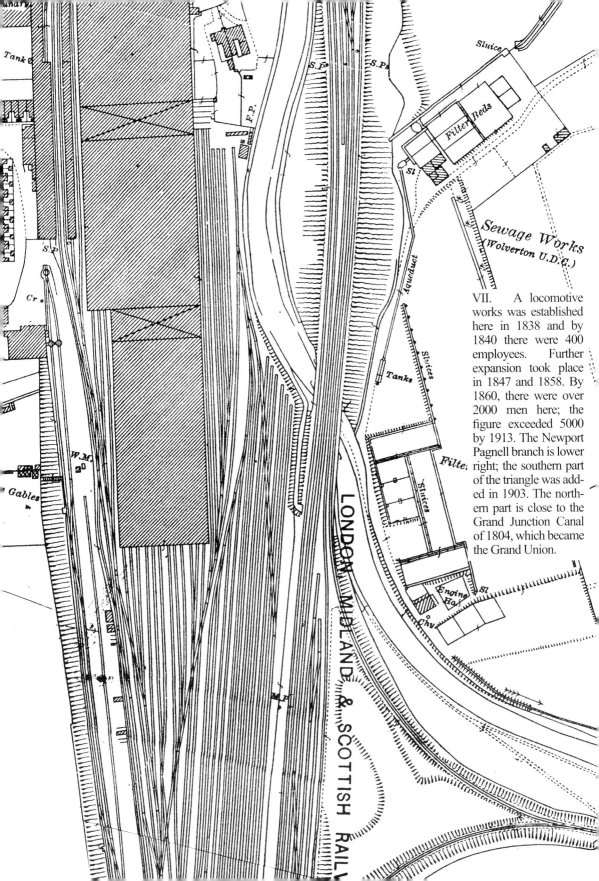

Tank

S.P.

S.P.

Sluice

Filter Beds

Sl.

Sewage Works
(Wolverton U.D.C.)

S.P.

Cr.

Aqueduct

Sluices

Tanks

W.M.

Filter

Gables

Sluices

Sl.

Engine Ho.

Chy.

LONDON MIDLAND & SCOTTISH RAILWAY

VII. A locomotive works was established here in 1838 and by 1840 there were 400 employees. Further expansion took place in 1847 and 1858. By 1860, there were over 2000 men here; the figure exceeded 5000 by 1913. The Newport Pagnell branch is lower right; the southern part of the triangle was added in 1903. The northern part is close to the Grand Junction Canal of 1804, which became the Grand Union.

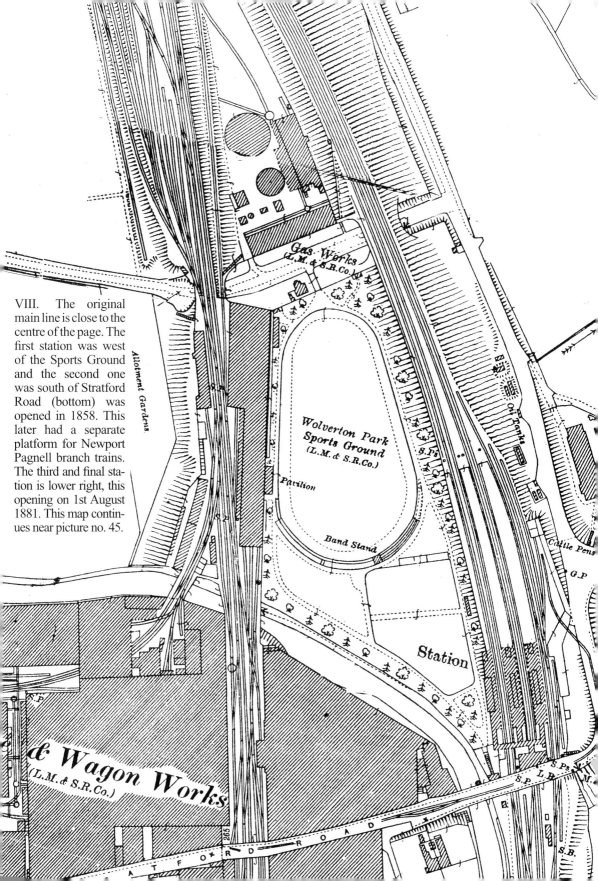

VIII. The original main line is close to the centre of the page. The first station was west of the Sports Ground and the second one was south of Stratford Road (bottom) was opened in 1858. This later had a separate platform for Newport Pagnell branch trains. The third and final station is lower right, this opening on 1st August 1881. This map continues near picture no. 45.

Allotment Gardens.

Gas Works
(L.M. & S.R.Co.)

Wolverton Park
Sports Ground
(L.M. & S.R.Co.)

Pavilion

Band Stand

Oil Tanks

S.P.

Cattle Pens

G.P.

Station

& Wagon Works
(L.M. & S.R.Co.)

S.P.

S.P.

S.P.
L.B.

S.B.

265

STRATFORD ROAD

WOLVERTON

16.   One of the five tram engines is seen outside the station, to the left of which is the doorway to the park. The tramway closed on 4th May 1926; the end of it is on map VIII in the goods yard. Three such cars were recorded behind one engine in some photographs. (Postcard)

17.   Standing at platform 5 on 18th May 1946 is 0-6-2T no. 7773 with the 12.15 Saturdays only to Newport Pagnell; the works had a 5½ day week at that time. On the right is the run-round loop. (H.C.Casserley)

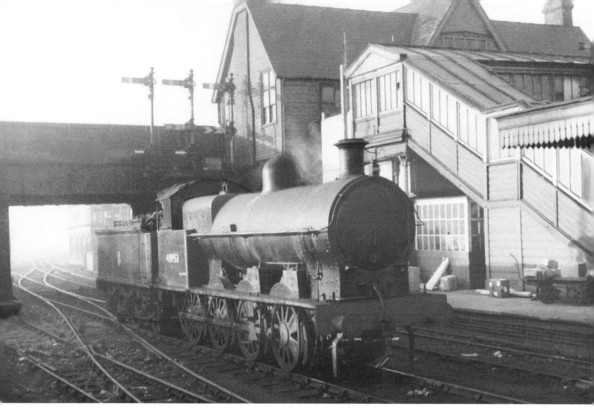

18.	"Super D" no. 48953 stands on the loop on 24th September 1955. There was a coal concentration depot here in 1967-72. (H.C.Casserley)

19.	The railway's park and sports grounds are seen from the top of the steps, with the station on the right and the works on the left. Old coaches provide accommodation. The area has been subjected to housing development in the 21st century. (J.Langford coll.)

20.   Local goods traffic ceased on 7th December 1970. The wires are up and so the end is nigh for BR class 5MT 4-6-0 no. 73038 and its train of Mk.I coaches. (D.Johnson)

21.   The station is seen not long before demolition in 1991. It had been gaslit until 1963, gas being made at the railway's own works; it is shown on map VIII. (British Rail)

22.   Cars were parked on the site of the bay platform and one siding in the distance served Amey Roadstone Corporation. All the buildings would soon vanish; one for gentlemen had already gone - see picture 20. (British Rail)

23.   The severe curvature of the deviation was reduced in 1973. This is the view from the steps on the left of the previous picture on 17th September 1992. The small ticket office is at the far end of the car park. The larger building is for telecommunication purposes. (D.A.Thompson)

WOLVERTON WORKS

←——— 24.   Carriage construction was centred here by the LNWR from 1862 when locomotive building was moved to Crewe. Shunting the Royal Train on 10th October 1954 is *Earlestown*, formerly LNWR no. 2359. (D.Trevor Rowe)

←——— 25.   There was earlier a fleet of four 0-6-0STs in use as service locos here, all having been rebuilt from LNWR tender engines. The signal box is now on the Northampton & Lamport Railway. (D.Johnson)

26.   This is North Yard, facing north in January 1957. The white objects are weighted point levers. (H.C.Casserley)

27.   Here is the view south, on the same day, of North Yard. (H.C.Casserley)

28. This was the route of the original main line and is seen on 23rd June 1962. Much of the site has been the subject of residential and commercial development. (P.J.Kelley)

29. Another view of the old main line is southwards, under Stratford Road, and includes the site of the second station beyond it. The first was behind the camera. (J.C.Gillham)

30.   Nos 29 to 32 were taken on 9th August 1970. This southward view is from near the centre of map VI. Uppermost is Blue Bridge, used simply to join fields. (J.C.Gillham)

31.   The line shafting and belts were still in use. This was thought to be the original locomotive erection shop of 1838. (J.C.Gillham)

32.   Photography of the Royal Train in its dedicated shed was seldom possible. No. 806 is on the left, no. 5155 middle and no. 2901 on the right. The train was still resident here in 2007. (J.C.Gillham)

33.   DC electrics are to be seen beyond the bogies on the right during the 1978 Open Day. Note the small turntables. The premises became part of Railcare Ltd on 6th May 1995, Alstom Railcare Ltd from 18th June 2001 and Railcare Ltd again from 1st February 2007. (D.Lovett)

Newport Pagnell Branch

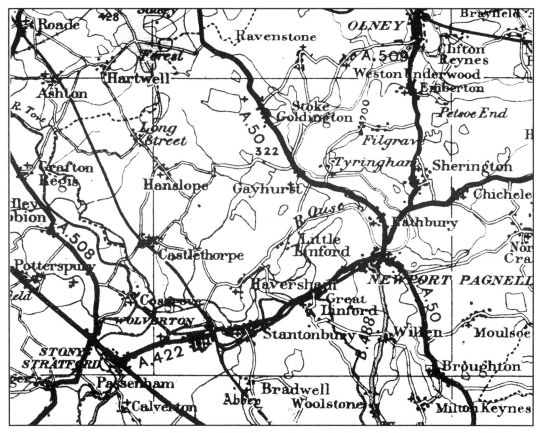

IX.   The 1946 survey at 2 miles to 1 inch shows the relationship of Olney to the branch, but not the earthworks or the bridge that were completed. The W&SS Tramway ran close to the A422. Lower right is Milton Keynes, which had a population of only 169 in 1961.

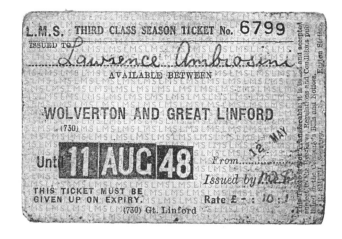

BRADWELL

34.   A classic posed postcard view includes a train from Wolverton passing under Bradwell Road. The district was originally known as Stantonbury. Only the platform remains.
(Lens of Sutton coll.)

X.   The private siding was added in 1870 and used for coal after the limeworks closed. The map includes the canal and is from 1900.

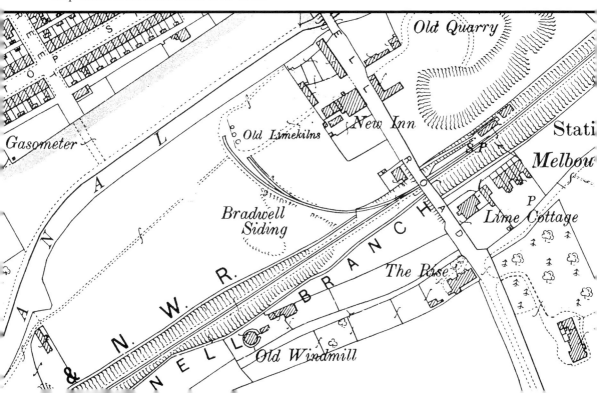

35.	The water tank was the only source of water for branch engines. This view towards the terminus is from April 1959. The branch formation has been adapted for cyclists and pedestrians. (R.M.Casserley)

36.	The private siding is evident; it was used by an oil company and a scrap metal merchant in the final years. The photograph is from 24th August 1964, just days before passenger service ceased. (J.C.Gillham)

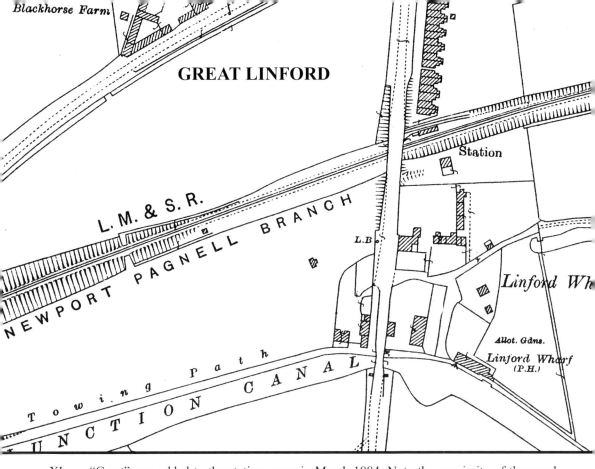

GREAT LINFORD

Blackhorse Farm

L.M. & S.R.

NEWPORT PAGNELL BRANCH

Station

L.B.

Towing Path

JUNCTION CANAL

Linford Wh

Allot. Gdns.

Linford Wharf (P.H.)

XI.　"Great" was added to the station name in March 1884. Note the proximity of the canal wharf. The station house, south of the platform, was added in 1878. This is the 1925 edition.

WOLVERTON and NEWPORT PAGNELL

Week Days only

Miles		a.m	a.m	a.m	a.m S	noon S	p.m	p.m	p.m	p.m
—	50 London (Euston) dep	..	6 40	7 25	1050	12 0	12A11	3 0	..	..
—	Wolverton .... dep	7 48	8 35	10 0	1225	1 33	2 40	4 50	5 43	..
1½	Bradwell	..	8 38	10 3	1228	1 36	2 43	4 53	5 46	..
2½	Great Linford	..	8 42	10 7	1232	1 40	2 47	4 57	5 51	..
4	Newport Pagnell .. arr	7 56	8 46	1011	1236	1 44	2 51	5 1	5 55	..

Week Days only

Miles		a.m	a.m	a.m	a.m S	p.m	p.m	p.m	p.m	p.m
—	Newport Pagnell.. dep	7 15	8 0	8 49	1140	1 0	1 50	4 5	5 17	6 8
1½	Great Linford	7 17	8 2	8 51	1142	1 2	1 52	4 7	5 19	6 5
2½	Bradwell	7 23	8 7	8 56	1147	1 7	1 57	4 12	5 24	6 10
4	Wolverton K ...... arr	7 29	8 11	9 0	1151	7 11	2 1	4 16	5 28	6 14
56½	50 London (Euston) arr	9√15	9 44	10 7	2 9	3ʄ37	3 38	6 19	..	8 13

1934 timetable

WOLVERTON and NEWPORT PAGNELL

Down.

Week Days only.

Miles		mrn	mrn		mrn	mrn S	mrn		aft	aft	aft	aft	aft		aft	aft	aft E	aft S	aft S	
—	412 London (Euston) .... dep	7 0	..		7 40	9 30	1040	..	12 5	1215	..	3 5	4 10	5 32	..	6 57	5 30	7 15	..	..
—	Wolverton .... dep	8 22	9 3	..	9 50	11 5	1215	..	1 32	2 15	3 04	25	4 57	0	..	7 45	9 59	1010	1025	1145
1	Bradwell J	8 25	9 11	..	9 55	11 8	1218	..	1 35	2 18	54	28	4 87	3	..	7 48	9 89	1013	1028	Kk
2½	Great Linford	8 29	9 15	..	10 2	1113	1228	..	1 40	2 23	12	33	5 55	7 8	..	7 53	9 12	1018	1033	1153
4	Newport Pagnell ...... arr	8 33	9 19	..	10 8	1118	1233	..	1 45	2 28	18	38	6 0	7 13	..	7 58	9 16	1023	1038	1159

Up.

Week Days only.

Miles		mrn	mrn	mrn		mrn	mrn S		aft S	aft E	aft S	aft	aft	aft	aft		aft	aft		aft
—	Newport Pagnell .... dep	7 25	8 45	9 22	..	1020	1140	..	1 0	5 1	5 0	2 35	4 55	20	6 10	7 18	..	8 25	9 18	..	9 50
1½	Great Linford	7 31	8 48	9 24	..	1024	1143	..	1 5	9 1	5 32	39	49 5	24	6 13	7 21	..	8 28	9 20	..	9 53
3	Bradwell J	7 38	8 53	9 29	..	1028	1148	..	1 12	14 1	58 2	44	54 5	29	6 18	7 26	..	8 33	9 25	..	9 58
4	Wolverton K 412, 425 arr	7 42	8 57	9 33	..	1032	1152	..	1 18	18 2	22 2	48	58 5	33	6 22	7 30	..	8 37	9 29	..	10 2
56½	425 London (Euston) .... arr	9 30	1015	1125 ⁿ	..	12 0	..	..	2 55	2 36	..	4	5 15ʄ33	..	7 50	..	..	1010	1135	..	..

E or E̸ Except Saturdays　　ʄ 1 mile to New Bradwell　　K Station for Stony Stratford (2 miles)

Kk Stops to set down　　ʟ Arr 5 20 aft on Mons & Sats　　ⁿ Arr 11 40 min on Sats　　S Sats only

1956 timetable

37.   No siding was provided here, probably due to the proximity of the canal wharf, where coal could be unloaded cheaply. The picture is from 1957; the platform was extant 50 years later. (Stations UK)

38.   A westward view from August 1964 includes staff transport. Less obvious, and to the rear of it, is a hand operated water pump for supply to the toilets. (J.C.Gillham)

NEWPORT PAGNELL

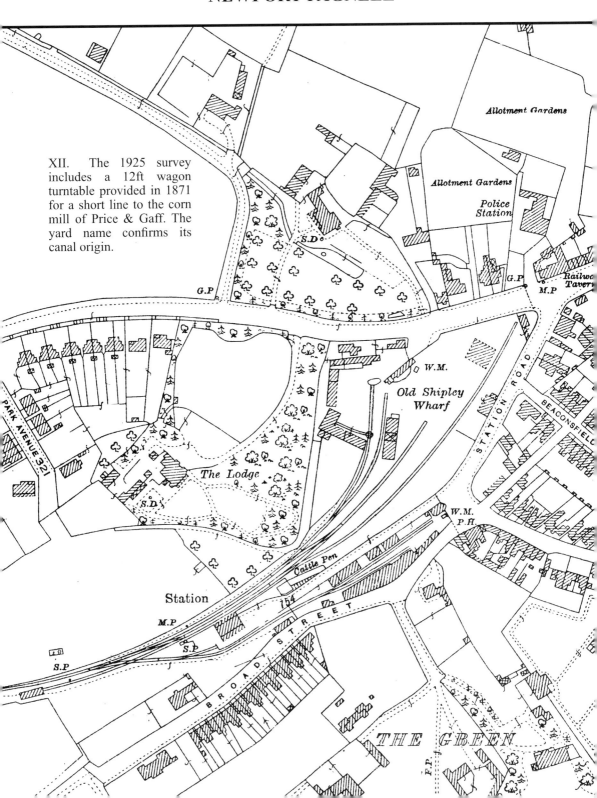

XII. The 1925 survey
includes a 12ft wagon
turntable provided in 1871
for a short line to the corn
mill of Price & Gaff. The
yard name confirms its
canal origin.

S.D

G.P

Allotment Gardens

Allotment Gardens

Police
Station

G.P
M.P

Railwa
Tavern

W.M.

Old Shipley
Wharf

STATION ROAD

BEACONSFIEL

PARK AVENUE 321

The Lodge

S.D

W.M.
P.H

Cattle Pen

Station

154

BROAD STREET

M.P

S.P

S.P

THE GREEN

F.P.

39.　　No. 27561 was one of the popular "Coal Tanks" and it is about to propel its coaches back to Wolverton at 1.12pm on 10th April 1948. The branch was normally operated in this manner. (H.C.Casserley)

40.　　Seen from the end of the platform in 1952 is the ground frame, the fixed home signal with small "calling on" arm and the engine shed. This closed on 15th June 1955 and had replaced the original (ex-Leighton Buzzard) one, which had been destroyed by fire on 1st January 1916. (A.J.Pike/F.Hornby coll.)

41.   The ground frame is also included in this view from the 1950s. The grounded van was used for sorting parcels. (Lens of Sutton coll.)

42.   The yard's five-ton crane is included in this panorama from 24th August 1964. Aston Martin cars were made in the town and were often loaded here. (J.C.Gillham)

43.   The east elevation was recorded on the same day. Parcels traffic was substantial to the end. The local population was about 4000 in 1900, the figure rising to just over 5000 by the time of closure. (J.C.Gillham)

44.   Standard class 2 2-6-2Ts were used in the final years of branch passenger service, but not all were fitted for push-pull working. The post carries an illuminated STOP sign, of value on foggy nights. This is 2-6-2T no. 41222, of LMS origin. (Stations UK)

45.   Locally, the train was affectionately known as the "Newport Nobby", but as the "Motor" by railwaymen. The driving compartment is shown clearly on almost the last day of service. (Millbrook House)

8491

L.M.&S.R. For
conditions see back
THIRD CLASS
SINGLE
Bradwell
Bradwell To
GREAT LINFORD
Great Linford

L.M.&S.R. For
conditions see back
THIRD CLASS
SINGLE
Bradwell
Great Linford

8491

·15½ Z   FARE ·15½ Z

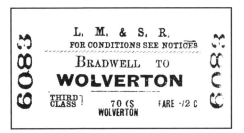

6083

L. M. & S. R.
FOR CONDITIONS SEE NOTICES

BRADWELL   TO
WOLVERTON

THIRD
CLASS   70 (S   FARE ·12 C
WOLVERTON

6083

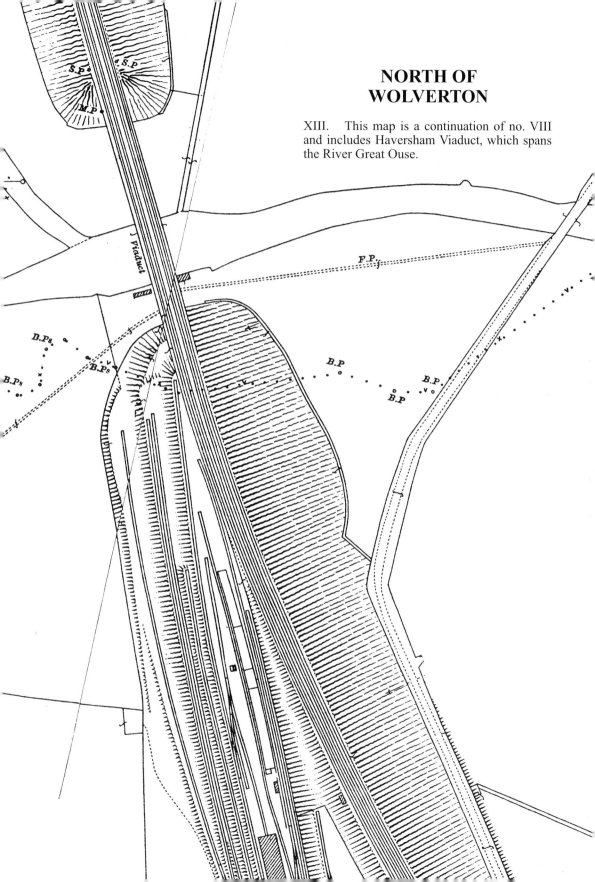

NORTH OF WOLVERTON

XIII.   This map is a continuation of no. VIII and includes Haversham Viaduct, which spans the River Great Ouse.

46.   The structure is also known as Wolverton Viaduct and was doubled in width in the mid-1870s. This view is from 1938. (R.M.Casserley coll.)

47.   With plenty of water available, the almost level valley was an ideal location in which to establish Castlethorpe water troughs. "Prince of Wales" class no. 1749 *Precedent* is running to Manchester in about 1925. (L.J.Thompson/E.Talbot)

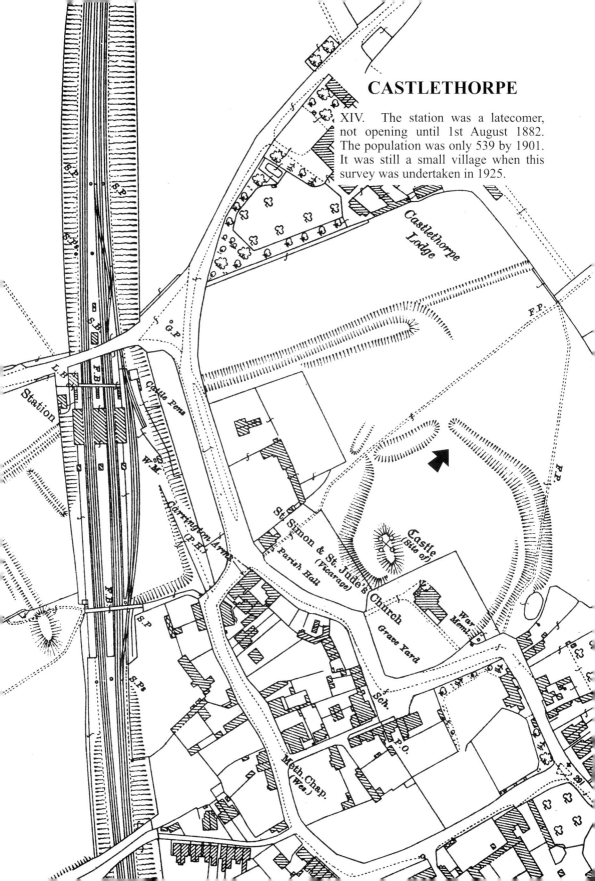

CASTLETHORPE

XIV. The station was a latecomer, not opening until 1st August 1882. The population was only 539 by 1901. It was still a small village when this survey was undertaken in 1925.

Castlethorpe Lodge

Station

Castle Pens

Carrington Arms (P.H.)

St. Simon & St. Jude's Church

Parish Hall (Vicarage)

Castle (Site of)

War Mem'l

Grave Yard

Sch.

P.O.

Meth. Chap. (Wes.)

F.P.

F.P.

48.   On the right is the office for the weighing machine, marked W.M. on the map. The ticket office is on the left and it is linked to the platforms by a footbridge. (Lens of Sutton coll.)

49.   No. 6104 *Scottish Borderer* races towards London with a good clean exhaust. On the left is the stationmasters house and the signal box can be seen beyond the bridge. (G.H.Soole/R.M.Casserley coll.)

50. Evident beyond the ticket office is part of the footbridge in this photograph from 9th November 1963. Passenger service was withdrawn on 7th September 1964, not long after the station had been modernised. (J.C.Gillham)

51. The goods yard is empty and closed on 6th April 1964. It had been provided with a 3-ton crane. The nearest bridge carries a public footpath. Parts of the platforms were still visible in 2007. (Stations UK)

ROADE

XV.   The 1931 survey is at 6ins to 1 mile and shows most of the length of Roade Cutting. The Northampton line diverges to the right at the top. The population was only 691 in 1901.

52.   A long freight from the north rumbles through sometime in the 1930s, when all the canopies were still complete. The first station had been about 200yds further north until the quadrupling work started in the early 1880s. (Stations UK)

53.   A view north in 1950 includes much of the goods yard, which had no shed or crane. The nearest bridge carried a footpath. (R.M.Casserley coll.)

54.   A 1955 panorama shows few chimneys when compared with picture 52. The main building had gone and the others had been simplified. (H.C.Casserley)

55.   Three photographs from August 1964 show the situation shortly before total closure. These dates are as for Castlethorpe. (J.C.Gillham)

56.   There was a brief period between the steam and electric eras when diesel traction predominated. No. D383 is passing an A35 van near the disused cattle dock. (J.C.Gillham)

57.   The inclined row of parked cars is on the left of this southward glimpse through the catenary awaiting energisation. The crossovers between the tracks were removed and replaced by the new high speed Hanslope Junction, three miles to the south, on 7th November 1971. Out of sight was a bridge over the tracks which carried the Bedford-Towcester line (1891-1958). There was a west-north connection between the two routes until 1917. (J.C.Gillham)

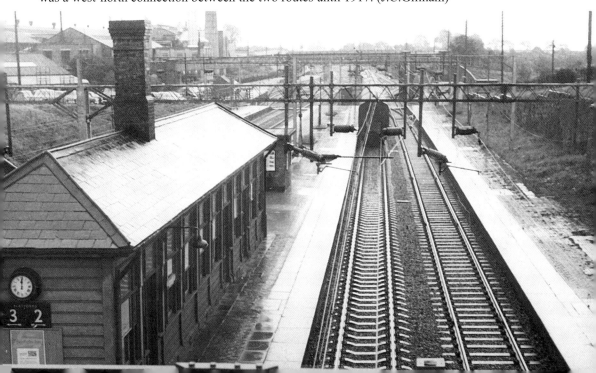

NORTH OF ROADE

58.   A coal train from the Midlands is
destined for London on 6th September 1947
and is on the 1881 Northampton route where
it converges with the 1838 main line (lower
left). Class 3F no. 4230 has passed through
Hunsbury Hill Tunnel (1152 yards long), four
miles north hereof. (L.Hanson/Ted Hancock)

⟶ 59.   A southward view in the same
vicinity shows that the Northampton lines were
constructed at a lower level and that the cutting sides
had to be supported by what is still known as "The
Birdcage". Working a down express on 29th July
1950 is no. 46156; its route continues in this volume
at picture 89. (L.Hanson/M.J.Stretton coll.)

SOUTH OF NORTHAMPTON

60.   The photographer is near West Bridge (above centre on the next map) looking south as two Stanier class 5 4-6-0s leave with "The Manxman" in the mid-1950s. Earl Cowpers Viaduct passes over the River Nene and the Grand Junction Canal - foreground. (A.W.V.Mace/Milepost 92½)

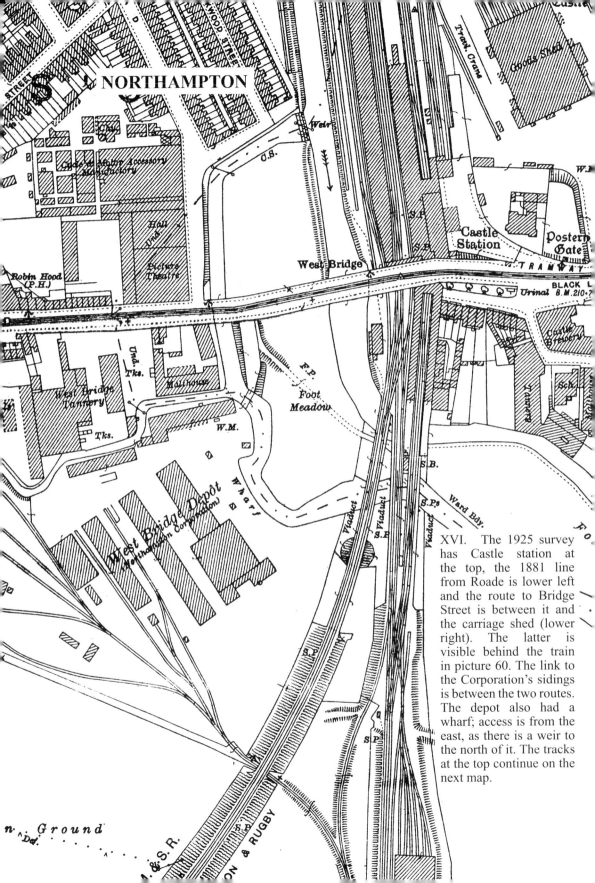

NORTHAMPTON

Cycle & Motor Accessory Manufactory

Robin Hood (P.H.)

West Bridge Tannery

Malthouse

Weir

C.S.

West Bridge

Foot Meadow

Castle Station

Postern Gate

TRAMWAY

BLACK L

Urinal B.M.210.7

Castle Brewery

West Bridge Depot
(Northampton Corporation)

Wharf

Viaduct

Viaduct

Viaduct

S.B.

S.P.

S.Ps.

Ward Bdy.

S.P.

XVI. The 1925 survey has Castle station at the top, the 1881 line from Roade is lower left and the route to Bridge Street is between it and the carriage shed (lower right). The latter is visible behind the train in picture 60. The link to the Corporation's sidings is between the two routes. The depot also had a wharf; access is from the east, as there is a weir to the north of it. The tracks at the top continue on the next map.

n. Ground

N. Dep.

L.&N.S.R.

ON & RUGBY

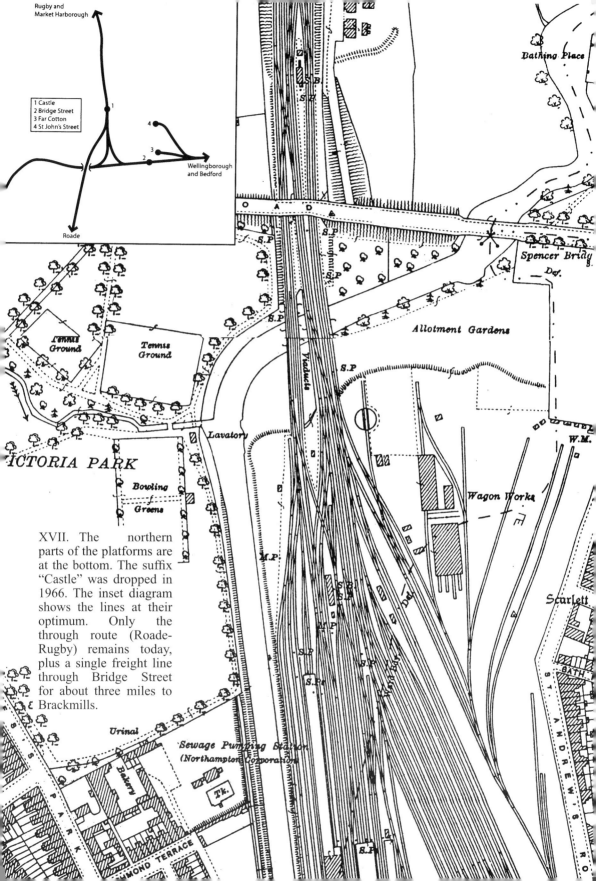

Rugby and
Market Harborough

1 Castle
2 Bridge Street
3 Far Cotton
4 St John's Street

Wellingborough
and Bedford

Roade

Bathing Place

S.B.
S.P.

R O A D

S.P.

S.P.

S.P.

Spencer Bridge

Def.

Tennis
Ground

Tennis
Ground

Allotment Gardens

S.P.

S.P.

Viaduct

S.P.

W.M.

Lavatory

ICTORIA PARK

Bowling
Greens

Wagon Works

Scarlett

XVII. The northern parts of the platforms are at the bottom. The suffix "Castle" was dropped in 1966. The inset diagram shows the lines at their optimum. Only the through route (Roade-Rugby) remains today, plus a single freight line through Bridge Street for about three miles to Brackmills.

M.P.

S.B.
S.P.

M.P.

BATH

S.P.

S.P.

Urinal

S.P.

Bakery

Sewage Pumping Station
(Northampton Corporation)

Tk.

ST ANDREW'S RO

PARK

S.P.

MOND TERRACE

61.   The east elevation made an impressive statement to the residents and the porte-cochère would have been appreciated by the gentry and their ladies alighting from their carriages.
(Lens of Sutton coll.)

62.   The former Midland Railway terminus at St. John Street was closed on 3rd July 1939 and all trains from Bedford terminated here thereafter. See *Bedford to Wellingborough* for that branch; its trains ran via Bridge Street station, which closed on 4th May 1964. This early postcard view of Castle station shows the low height of the platforms which facilitated wheel tapping.
(Lens of Sutton coll.)

63. The autotrain to Blisworth is seen behind 2-4-2T no. 26616 on 18th May 1946. This service was withdrawn on 4th January 1960, but the route was used for diversions during electrification work until 3rd January 1966. (H.C.Casserley)

64. Seen from platform 6 in 1954 is the up through platform, numbered 1. Beyond it are bays for trains to and from the north. No. 6 became No. 2 following electrification. (Stations UK)

65.   Looking from the north end of the platform, we witness 0-8-0 no. 49366 passing No. 2 Box, which closed on 3rd December 1982. Spencer Bridge Road crosses the tracks in the background. It spans the top of map XVII. (R.M.Casserley coll.)

66.   The two southern bays are near the centre of map XVI and about to depart on 24th September 1955 is 2-6-2T no. 41270 with the 2.53pm to Bedford. The through lines are on the left, the down island platform being beyond the bridge pier. It is now numbered 2 and 3. (H.C.Casserley)

67.   A complete transformation had taken place by the time that this photograph was taken in 1970. The main elevation faced south, instead of east. Behind it were two bay platforms (nos 4 and 5) and two docks. The work was undertaken in 1965-67. (Stations UK)

68.   Platform 1 was photographed from no. 2 on 22nd January 2003 as a class 321/4 unit approaches. These sets were used by both Silverlink and First Great Eastern at that time. (P.Jones)

69.   Recorded on the same day was Royal Mail unit no. 325014. The design was based on the class 319 passenger units. The 16 four-car units were built in Derby in 1995. (P.Jones)

70.   The headquarters for Siemens Rolling Stock Maintenance in the UK was established north of the station and the depot was officially opened on 27th June 2006. The five-road workshop would maintain the entire fleet of 30 class 350 Desiro EMUs, introduced in June 2005. (Siemens)

XVIII. The previous map continues on the left (lower). The point of separation of the two routes is on the right, but they ran parallel northwards for two miles from the station. In 2007 there were three running lines for almost two miles north of the station. On the west side was Siemens Depot, a down goods loop and three engineers sidings. On the east side there were five up sidings (loops), a reception line, 14 sidings in Castle Yard, plus three for La Farge Aggregates depot, which had been opened in February 1998 by Redlands. The signal box on the right was known as No. 4 Junction.

GBY

TRAMWAY

S.P

S.P

S.P

S.Ps

Saw Mill

Chy.

Brick Works

Crane

S.P

Timber Yard

S.Ps

ns

L.M. & S.R. NORTHAMPTON & MARKET HARBOROUGH

L.M. & S.R. ROADE, NORTHAMPTON & RUGB

S.P

S.P

S.P

CHURCH BRAMPTON

71.   The platforms had a short life, opening on 13th May 1912 and closing on 18th May 1931. They were mainly used by golfers, who had mostly defected to the motor car by that time. The station was also closed in 1917-19. The remains are seen during the electrification work. (Lens of Sutton coll.)

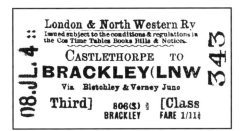

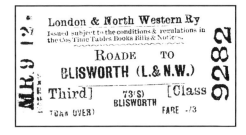

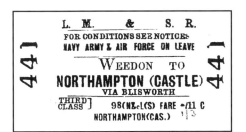

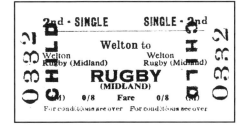

ALTHORP PARK

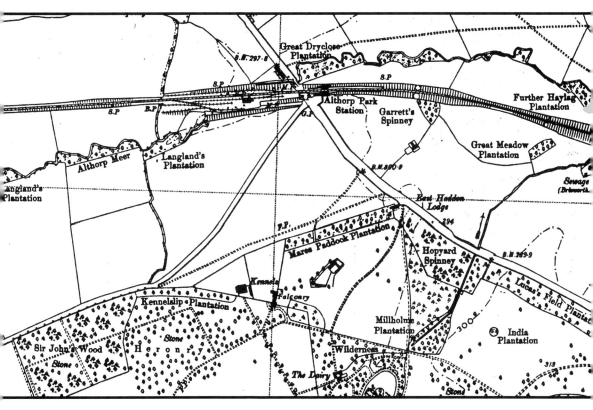

XIX.   The station was provided on the Spencer family's estate, but there was little habitation nearby. This is revealed on the 6 ins to 1 mile map of 1951.

72.   The station was the subject for an early postcard which has been damaged. However, it does show the relationship of the signal box to the platforms. (Lens of Sutton coll.)

73.	A view from 1959 includes the impressive south elevation, together with the photographer's Hillman 10. (H.C.Casserley)

XX.	The 1926 survey indicates a generous provision of facilities, largely for the estate. The crane shown was rated at 10 tons.

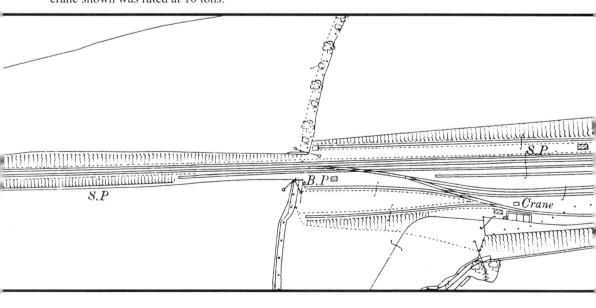

74.   Running in on 25th July 1959 is 4-6-0 no. 44712 with the 12.20pm Euston to Birmingham stopping train. Wooden platforms were employed to minimise the weight on the embankment. (H.C.Casserley)

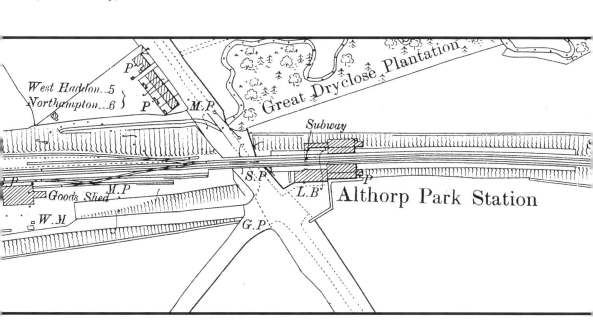

75.   Flat bottom rails had reached here by 1959, but oil lamps were still employed. The foot crossing was provided for staff, a subway being available for passengers; they had use of the station until 13th June 1960. It was demolished in 1962. (H.C.Casserley)

76.   Running east on 4th March 1961 is class 8F 2-8-0 no. 48748; the train is passing the long headshunt. Goods traffic continued here until 1st June 1964. The signal box closed on 15th Bebruary 1965. (Millbrook House)

LONG BUCKBY

XXI. Careful examination of the 1926 survey will show that the passenger station is entirely on the opposite side of the road from the goods yard. Like the other stations on the 1881 section, there was a 10-ton crane.

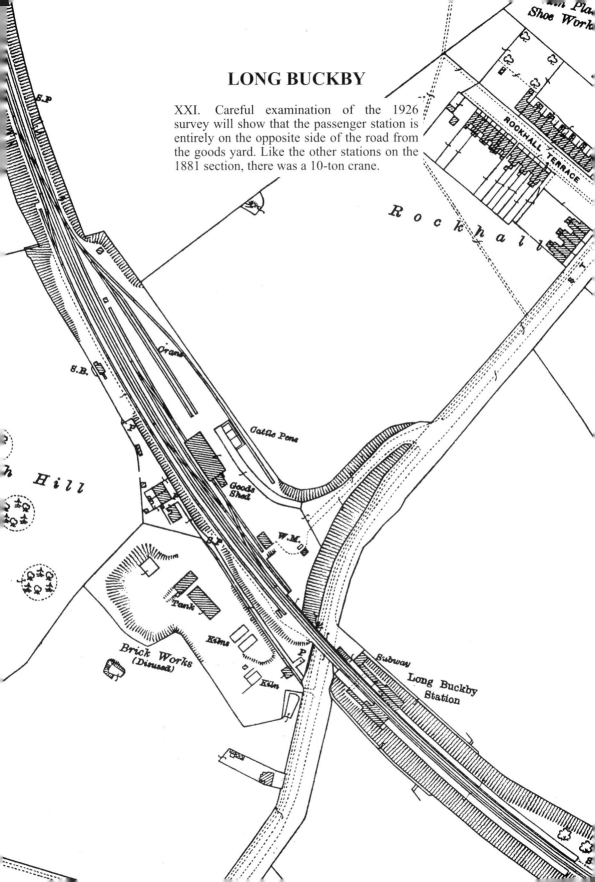

Rockhall

ROCKHALL TERRACE

Shoe Work

S.P

S.B.

Crane

Cattle Pens

Goods Shed

W.M.

Hill

Tank

Brick Works (Disused)

Kilns

Kiln

Subway

Long Buckby Station

77.   Sweeping round the curve by the goods shed is an up train, which is about to pass over the subway. Stock stands in the down refuge siding. There was a staff of 12 in the 1920s. (Lens of Sutton coll.)

78.   The view towards Northampton in 1959 includes well tended flower tubs and electric lighting. Back in 1901, a local population of 2147 had been recorded. (H.C.Casserley)

79.   This is from the same view point as picture 77, but is from 10th April 1965. Many old canopies could not tolerate the air turbulence of the new trains. Goods traffic ceased here on 29th April 1968. (R.M.Casserley)

80.   Two photographs from the same day complete our survey. The down side had a fully enclosed stairway from the subway to the arch-supported timber building. (R.M.Casserley)

81.   On the up side was the ticket office, which was fully staffed until May 1969. This was the only station between Northampton and Rugby not to suffer total closure. (R.M.Casserley)

82.   Facilities were minimal when the station was photographed in May 1992. The world's media focused on the station on 6th September 1997, following the funeral of Diana, Princess of Wales, and her subsequent burial at Althorp Park. The Royal Train and a fleet of Rolls-Royces were present that day. (D.A.Thompson)

KILSBY & CRICK

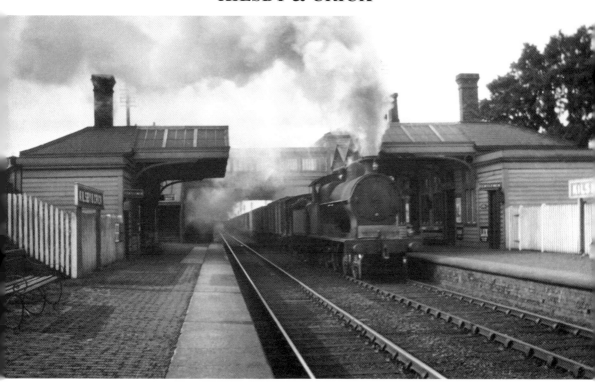

83.   No details are available, but it may be the 1930s. Kilsby had 475 residents in 1901 and Crick 613. The figures were only 666 and 780 respectively in 1961. (Stations UK)

84.   Several ex-LNWR coaches were used as dormitories by the permanent way engineers, but the date was not noted. Goods traffic ceased here on 3rd May 1965. (A.W.V.Mace/Milepost 92½)

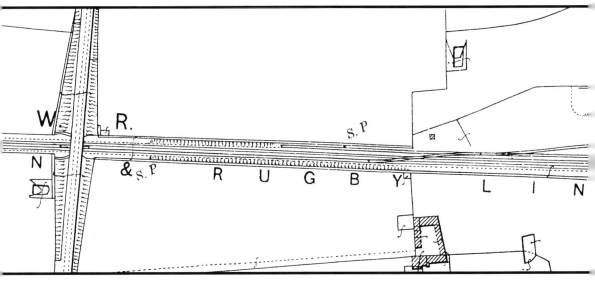

W R.

N

& s.P

S.P

R U G B Y LIN

XXII.   The 1900 survey again shows station and goods yard separated by a road. The 10-ton crane is not marked, as it presumably came later. The road near the station became the A5 in 1919.

85.   Long shorn of its canopies, the station seemed in good order when photographed on 25th July 1959. The enclosed footbridge and staircases were a luxury at such a little-used station. Work on a freight distribution depot began in the distance in the mid-1990s. (H.C.Casserley)

KILSBY & CRICK

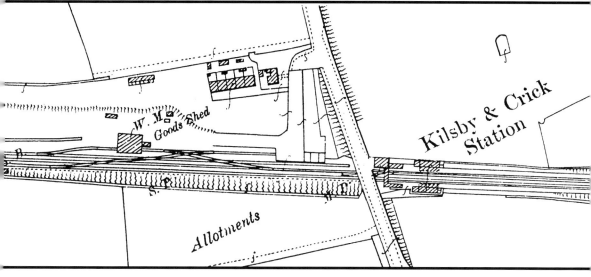

86.   The tiny booking hall was photographed on the same day and was closed, along with the station, on 1st February 1960. The letter box was probably even less used. Crick Tunnel (595yds) and Watford Lodge Tunnel (115yds) were south of the station. (H.C.Casserley)

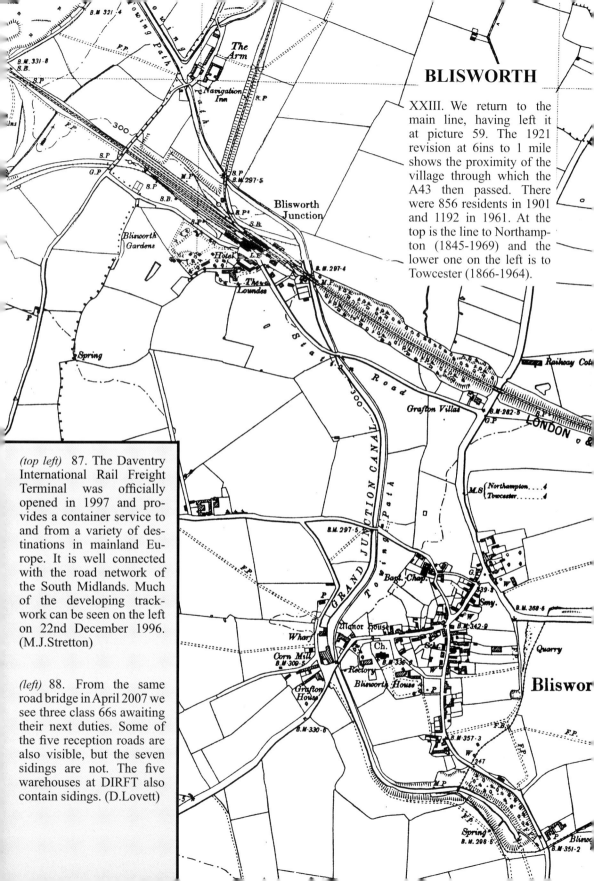

BLISWORTH

XXIII. We return to the main line, having left it at picture 59. The 1921 revision at 6ins to 1 mile shows the proximity of the village through which the A43 then passed. There were 856 residents in 1901 and 1192 in 1961. At the top is the line to Northampton (1845-1969) and the lower one on the left is to Towcester (1866-1964).

(top left) 87. The Daventry International Rail Freight Terminal was officially opened in 1997 and provides a container service to and from a variety of destinations in mainland Europe. It is well connected with the road network of the South Midlands. Much of the developing trackwork can be seen on the left on 22nd December 1996. (M.J.Stretton)

(left) 88. From the same road bridge in April 2007 we see three class 66s awaiting their next duties. Some of the five reception roads are also visible, but the seven sidings are not. The five warehouses at DIRFT also contain sidings. (D.Lovett)

89.   Bound for Euston with a very long train is LNWR "George V" class 4-4-0 no. 1623 *Nubian*. The train engine is a "Claughton" 4-6-0. The photograph was taken during the coal strike of 1921 and it reveals other destinations from here. (L.J.Thompson/R.S.Carpenter coll.)

90.   A 1959 picture includes the renamed Grand Union Canal and the massive water tank at the London end of the platforms. The Banbury service had been reduced to two trains per day towards the end. (R.M.Casserley)

91.   A view towards Roade in 1960 includes the rails round the steps to the subway and the crossovers used by branch trains, also diverted ones. The first station was ½ mile further south until about 1853. (Stations UK)

92.   Another 1960 photograph and this includes the curve to Northampton on the right. Its passenger dates are given in caption 63. The English Electric Type 4 speeding towards London eventually became class 40. (Stations UK)

93.   Passenger service was withdrawn on 4th January 1960 and goods followed on 6th July 1964. However, the sign was still in place when this photograph was taken on 24th August 1964. Only the nearby hotel is still standing. (J.C.Gillham)

NORTH OF BLISWORTH

94.   No. 5979 Frobisher races along near Gayton Brickworks Siding (left) and Banbury Lane signal box, in about 1929. In the background are the signals for the two Heyford loops. The location is top left on the map. Three miles further north was Heyford North signal box, where a siding for an ironworks was provided in 1870. (L.J.Thompson/E.Talbot coll.)

95.   No. 87007 *City of Manchester* heads north with a Virgin Trains service on 3rd May 2003. The class 87 locos were built at Crewe in 1973-75 and most of the 36 were designed for 110mph running. (M.Turvey)

96.   While lineside cabling is in progress, a Virgin class 390 "Pendolino" set speeds south on 28th July 2003. Built by Alstom in Birmingham, the welded aluminium tilting sets were designed for 140mph running. (M.Turvey)

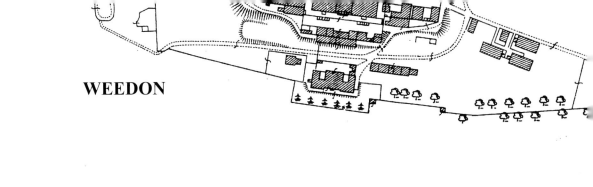

WEEDON

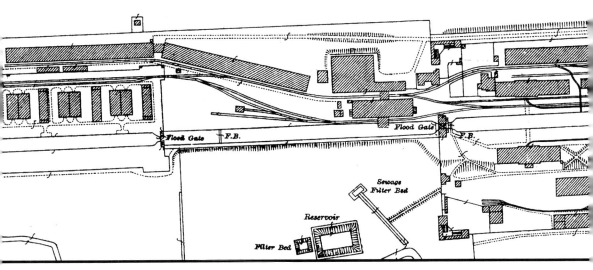

XXIV. After passing through Stowe Hill Tunnel (491yds), passengers were confronted by the Weedon Barracks complex of which the three main buildings have been preserved. Conceived as the last redoubt in the event of a French invasion during the Napoleonic Wars, this site was chosen for its distance from the coast and the communications offered by the Grand Junction Canal - which had reached Weedon Bec in 1796 - and the London-Chester Turnpike. The 1926 map at 20ins to 1 mile has the original route of the main line on the right and this included a drawbridge over the canal arm to the barracks.

97.   The view from the road bridge confirms that a goods line ran behind the up platform. Weedon Bec had a population of 1868 in 1901. (Lens of Sutton coll.)

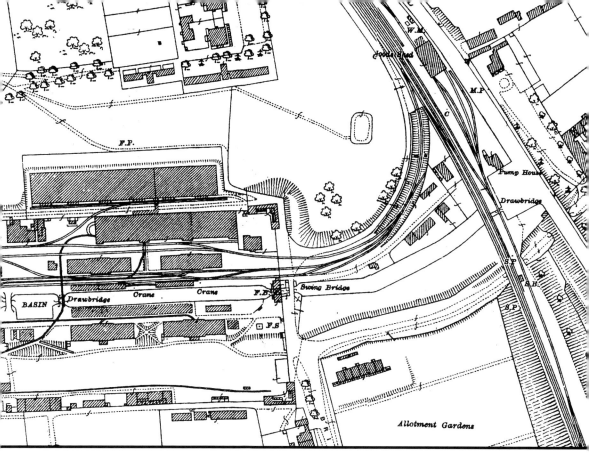

98.   A northward view in 1958 includes the bay platform and a push-pull train for Daventry and Leamington Spa. This service ceased and the station closed to passengers on 15th September 1958. The brick-built shelters were less than ten years old. (Stations UK)

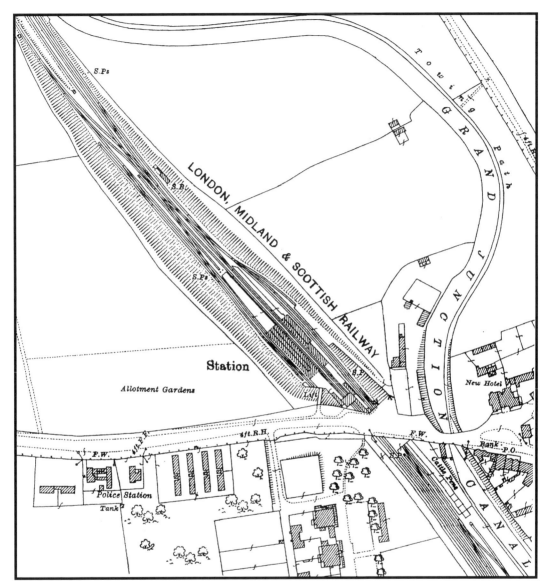

XXV. This map overlaps the previous one and features the station, which was completed in 1888 with the opening of the LNWR's new route to Leamington Spa. The previous station had been south of the road. The new main lines were raised to avoid the need for a drawbridge, but an old one was retained as a parallel siding. It is seen on the previous map, along with No. 1 Box, which was mostly switched out until abolished in 1957. The single line to Daventry is on the left at the top; a refuge siding is on the right.

99.   There were intermediate boxes north hereof at Brockhall and Buckby Bank until 9th December 1934. This July 1959 view south includes part of the goods yard; this was in use until 3rd May 1965. Freight continued to Daventry until 1963. No. 2 Box was operational until 26th September 1964 and the siding to the Barracks until 2nd August 1965. (H.C.Casserley)

100.   High security restricted photography during military use. Evidence of the sidings had re-emerged through the tarmac in 2007. The disused canal basin is on the left. (D.Lovett)

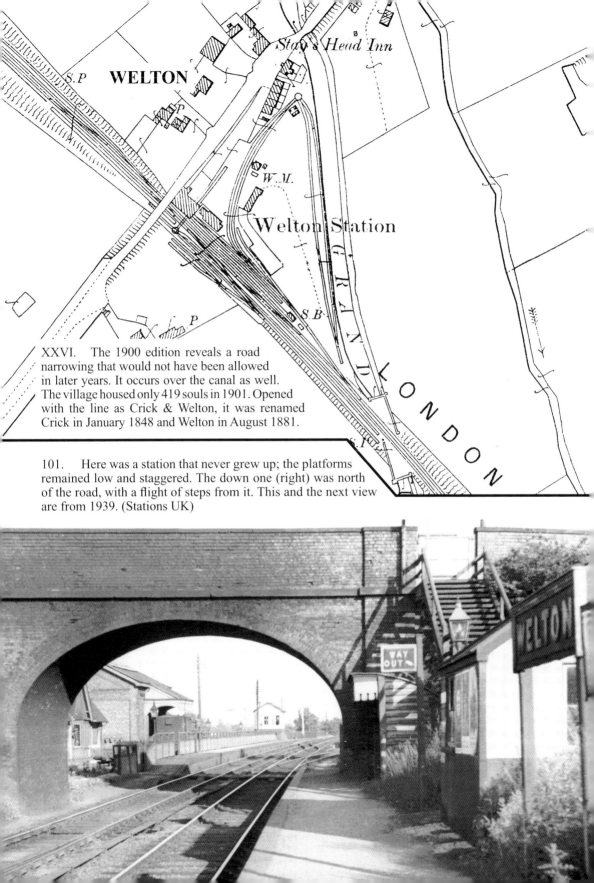

S.P

WELTON

Stag's Head Inn

P

W.M.

Welton Station

S.B.

P

GRAND

LONDON

S.P.

XXVI. The 1900 edition reveals a road narrowing that would not have been allowed in later years. It occurs over the canal as well. The village housed only 419 souls in 1901. Opened with the line as Crick & Welton, it was renamed Crick in January 1848 and Welton in August 1881.

101. Here was a station that never grew up; the platforms remained low and staggered. The down one (right) was north of the road, with a flight of steps from it. This and the next view are from 1939. (Stations UK)

WAY OUT

WELTON

102.   A southward panorama from the road bridge does not include the crane, as it was in the goods shed. It was rated at 25cwt. The up platform is in the centre, devoid of even a seat. (Stations UK)

103.   The station closed on 7th July 1958, but the goods yard was in use until 1st June 1964. The photograph is from July 1959 and includes the long up refuge siding. (H.C.Casserley)

NORTH OF WELTON

104.   Kilsby Tunnel presented incredible difficulties in its making, 26 men losing their lives in the task. As with Roade cutting, unexpected water was struck, but continuous pumping day and night with up to 13 pumps for eight months finally won the day. Thirty six million bricks were used in its construction over a period of four years. (D.Ibbotson/R.S.Carpenter coll.)

105.   The two flashes of light noticed on the way through are from the two 60 foot diameter ventilating shafts, one of which is 120 feet deep. There are six other smaller shafts. The tunnel length is currently quoted as 1 mile 656 yds. It opened three years before Box Tunnel, where death by asphyxiation was still being forecast for travellers. (D.Ibbotson/R.S.Carpenter coll.)

SOUTH OF RUGBY

106.   An up express via Northampton runs on the embankment as it leaves Rugby on 16th July 1960. Hillmorton box lasted until the panel at Rugby came into use on 20th September 1964. There was no connection between the two routes, but there were up goods loops on both. (R.S.Carpenter)

107.   This is Clifton Road Junction (see map XXVIII) and running on the down Northampton line with an excursion is no. 73020. The down main line is in the foreground; the up one passes under the steel span. This undated view has the single line curve from Clifton Mill behind the third coach. The flying junction was completed in 1885. (A.W.V.Mace/Mile Post 92½)

108.   Near the junction on the right of the next map is running an LNWR "Precursor" 4-6-0, bound for London. The GCR spans are in the left background. The Loop Line divides into a goods and a platform road west of the road bridge. This box lasted until 1939. (R.M.Casserley coll.)

London & North Western Ry.
Issued subject to the conditions & regulations in the Coy Time Tables Books Bills & Notices
CHILD
ALTHORP PARK TO
NORTHAMPTON (CASTLE)
Thir   [Class
.) FARE -/3½
06 AP 13   4870

London & North Western Ry.
RUGBY
3 PLATFORM C
This ticket must be given up when leaving the Station or at the time of booking.
AP 11 C   5388

RUGBY

River Avon

U.D. By.
Filter Beds

Allotment
Gardens

B.M. 283·2

Water Works
(Rugby U.D.C.)
Reservoir

Engine
Shed

Brownsover Mill
(Disused)

286·6

305

Reservoir
Rugby U.D.C.

Old Canal

500 Yds.

Clifton Mill

Liable to Floods

Clifton
Old Wharf
(Disused)

Clift.
Clift. St.

Viaduct

Spring

Clifton Brook

Canal (Disused)

Spring

Wagon
Works

298·4

L. & N. W. R.
RUGBY & STAMFORD

Fairwood
Cottages

Vicarage

Goods Engine Shed

L. & N. W. Station

Patterdales

P.O.
(Sorting)

300·7

316

B.M. 313·9

Clifton
New Wharf

Butler's Leap

L. & N. W. R.
LOOP LINE

U.D. By.

Viaduct

Liable to Floods

Rugby School
Golf Course

Laundry

B.M. 348·9

Club House

Viaduct

350

Clifton Road
Junction

B.M. 373·7

SPOILBANK

Allotment Gardens

Liable to Floods

300

Golf
Club House

Rugby Fields

LONDON & NORTH WE

374·5

L.B.

St. Peter's Church

370·6

Lodge

School

381·7

Mortuary
Mort. Chap.

CEMETERY

Mort. Chap.

RUGBY

B.M. 385·4

Eastlands

Spring

B.P.

Workho.
Hospital

LOWER HILLMORTON ROAD

Lamp
Works

389·4

386·3

Benn Farm

G.C. Station

GREAT CENTRAL RAILWAY

M
Rifle Range

389

384

U.D. By.

B.P.

Allotment
Gardens

Pump House
(Rugby U.D.C.
Sewage Works)

Southfields

S.B.

B.M. 387·3

W

380·0

Benn Farm

Rugby
Stud Farm

XXVII. Our route comes in on the right of this 1922 map at 6 ins to 1 mile. The station at the bottom is featured in our *Aylesbury to Rugby* album. The site of the first station is beyond the left border. The second one (c.1840-85) was a little west of the one marked. The development of the lines at Rugby has already been outlined at the start of this volume. The town has been the home of the famous Rugby School since 1567. It was there in 1823 that the rules of football were amended to create a new game.

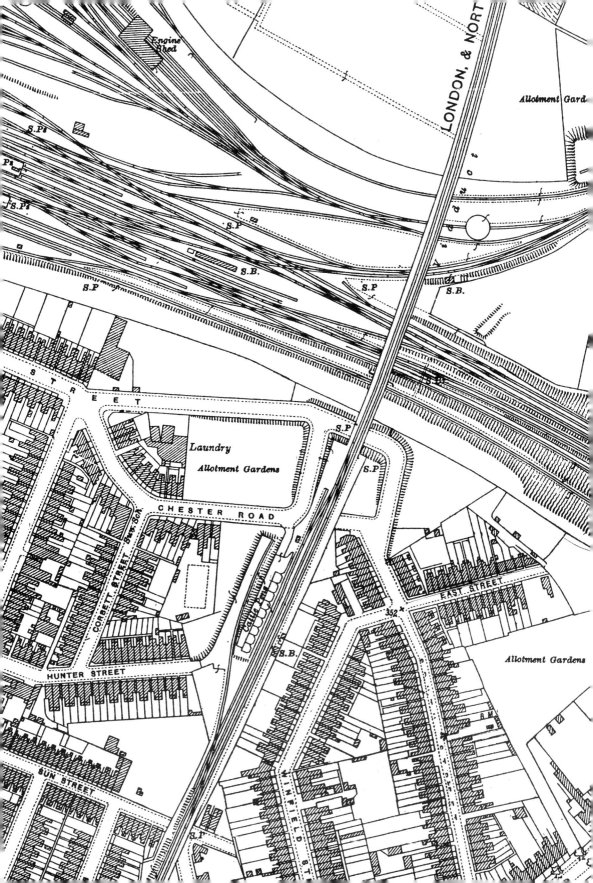

Engine
Shed

S.P.

P.

S.P.

S.P.

LONDON. & NOR

Allotment Gard

S.B.

S.P

S.P.

S.B.

S.P

S.P.

STREET

Laundry

Allotment Gardens

CHESTER ROAD

S.P.

S.P.

EAST STREET

CORBETT STREET

Sun. Sch.

Cable Lane

352

Allotment Gardens

HUNTER STREET

S.B.

WINFIELD ST.

SUN STREET

R.M.

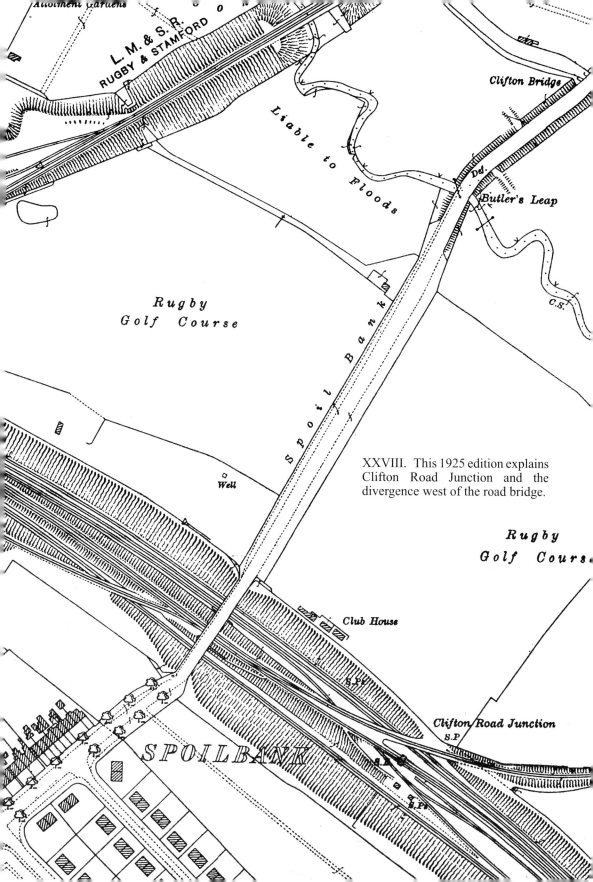

Allotment Gardens

L. M. & S. R.
RUGBY & STAMFORD

Clifton Bridge

Liable to Floods

Dd.

Butler's Leap

Rugby
Golf Course

Spoil Bank

C.S.

Well

XXVIII. This 1925 edition explains
Clifton Road Junction and the
divergence west of the road bridge.

Rugby
Golf Cours

Club House

S.P.

Clifton Road Junction
S.P

SPOILBANK

S.P.

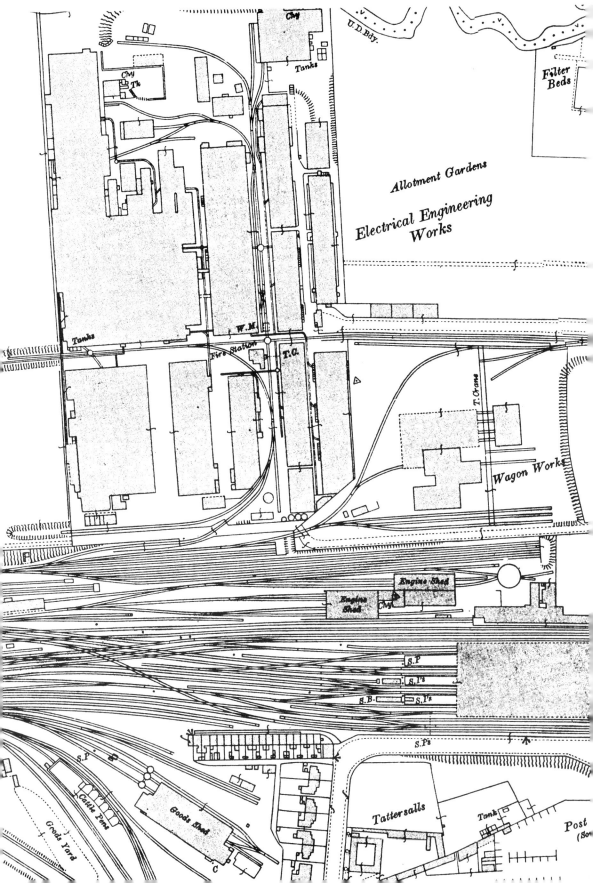

Chy

Tanks

Chy
Tk

U.D.Bdy.

Filter
Beds

Allotment Gardens

Electrical Engineering
Works

Tanks

W.M.

Fire Station

T.O.

T. Crane

Wagon Works

Engine Shed

Engine
Shed

Chy

S.P.

S.P's

S.B.

S.P's

S.P's

S.P.

Cattle Pens

Goods Shed

Goods Yard

C

Tattersalls

Tank

Post
(Sou

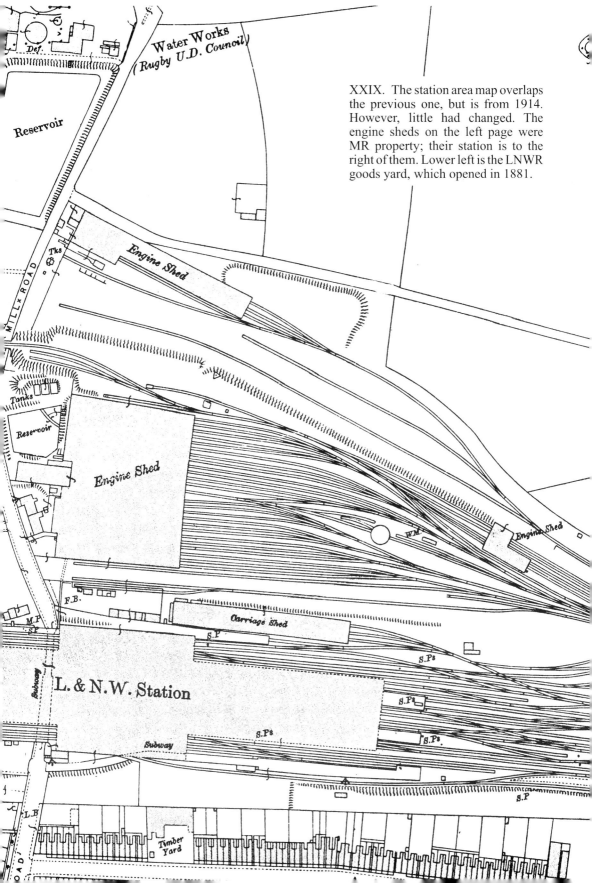

Water Works
(Rugby U.D. Council)

Reservoir

XXIX. The station area map overlaps the previous one, but is from 1914. However, little had changed. The engine sheds on the left page were MR property; their station is to the right of them. Lower left is the LNWR goods yard, which opened in 1881.

Engine Shed

Tks

M I L L × R O A D

Tanks

Reservoir

Engine Shed

Engine Shed

W.M.

F.B.

M.P.

Carriage Shed

S.P.

S.Ps

L. & N.W. Station

Subway

Subway

S.Ps

S.Ps

S.Ps

S.P

L.B.

Timber Yard

ROAD

109.   A "Precursor" class was recorded leaving Rugby with LNWR stock. It is passing under a northbound GCR train and is running near the incline down from the span in the centre of the previous picture. The impressive signal gantry stood from 1898 to 1939. (R.M.Casserley coll.)

110.   The departure board is showing "Coventry & Birmingham", while the news hoarding suggests a World War I date. The second finger board lists other destinations for the next train. (Lens of Sutton coll.)

111.   A photograph from almost the same location on 7th July 1956 features 4-6-2 no. 46200 *The Princess Royal* coming in with "The Mid-Day Scot". The roof survived World War II fairly intact. (A.W.V.Mace/Mile Post 92½)

112.   The location of the large engine shed is shown on the map. This handicapped 0-6-0 was recorded on 24th June 1956. The shed was 2A and 106 locomotives were allocated in 1950. It was re-roofed in 1955; Shed 2 had 11 roads and was used for light repairs, while the running shed had 12 roads. The sheds closed on 25th May 1965. (H.C.Casserley)

113.   Opened near the former GCR bridge on 19th October 1948 was the BR Testing Station. It was only used 46 times in 11 years and dismantled in 1970. The building was demolished in 1984. (A.W.V.Mace/Mile Post 92½)

114.   No. 70044 *Earl Haig*, a BR Standard 4-6-2, is departing for Manchester in about 1956. It is passing No. 4 Box, which had 84 levers; No. 1 was at the south end of the station and had a 185-lever frame. The boxes closed on 13th September 1964, the new power box having opened on the 7th. (A.W.V.Mace/Mile Post 92½)

115. The term "Rugby Midland" is seen over the entrance on 9th March 1959. It was used from 1st January 1948 until 3rd May 1970. (P.Kingston)

116. LMS-designed and BR-built, 2-6-2T no. 41278 waits to depart for Leamington Spa on 13th April 1959. One gas light is on as the shadows lengthen. Rugby replaced Nuneaton as the southern limit of electric services on 30th November 1964. (G.D.King/M.J.Stretton coll.)

MP Middleton Press

EVOLVING THE ULTIMATE RAIL ENCYCLOPEDIA

Easebourne Lane, Midhurst, West Sussex.
GU29 9AZ   Tel:01730 813169

www.middletonpress.co.uk   email:info@middletonpress.co.uk
A-9780906520   B-9781873793   C-9781901706   D-9781904474

OOP Out of print at time of printing - Please check availability   BROCHURE AVAILABLE SHOWING NEW TITLES